It's All About

Time Management

Niurka Castaneda

Published by
Niurka Castaneda
Copyright © 2021 Niurka Castaneda

Books by AMOR umbrella Publishers can be acquire for educational, commercial or promotional use. For information about special discounts for bulk purchases, please contact AMOR umbrella Publishers, Miami, FL 33177 at bulk@amorumbrella.com.
AMOR umbrella is a registered trademark of Ventures C & A LLC.
AMOR umbrella Speakers Bureau can bring authors to your live event. For more information or to book an event, contact the AMOR umbrella Speakers Bureau at speak@amorumbrella.com or amorumbrella.com. The information provided in this book is for informational purposes only and is not intended to be a source of advice or credit analysis with respect to the material presented. The information and/or documents contained in this book do not constitute legal or financial advice and should never be used without first consulting with a financial or legal professional to determine what may be best for your individual needs.

Softcover ISBN: 978-1-7364815-3-0
Ebook ISBN: 978-1-7364815-4-7
Hardcover ISBN: 979-8-9855579-8-5
Library of Congress Control Number: 2022915548
ISSN Pending Application APPL100005103
Cover Design: Alejandro Castaneda
Interior: Niurka Castaneda
Printed by Ventures C & A LLC in the United States of America
1st Edition 1 MAR 2022
AMOR umbrella
Miami, FL 33177
www.amorumbrella.com

Dedication & Acknowledgement

For my family,

for each and every person who has helped me believe in myself, in a

mission greater than myself, in the great potential each of us has and to the

most authentic, creative, bravest people I know: The Entrepreneurs of the

World.

It's All About Time Management Checklist	PG	Not Done	Done
INTRODUCTION	6		
1 FINDING TIME	10		
2 MANAGE YOUR TIME	20		
3 SET GOALS	38		
4 SCHEDULE IT	44		
5 COLOR IT	48		
6 ELIMINATE OR REDUCE	52		

INTRODUCTION

Starting a business involves planning, making key financial decisions, investing your time and resources in an efficient way that allows you to grow. **It's All about Time Management**© will take you through simple practical steps to figure out when you are the most productive on specific tasks and allow you to create a framework for optimal productivity that can help you master your time. It will also provide the necessary strategies & tools to work smarter and get more done in less time.

This Book is part of the series: **"How to Launch the Business that Fits Your Lifestyle"**, a one stop resource guide to help you get a comprehensive understanding of what is required to build the lifestyle of your dreams. It will empower you with the critical skills, thoughts, feelings, strategies, relevant information, and actions you need to adopt to be successful in your endeavors. Each book can be read independently of the others..

Hey there!

> *"Time is a created thing. To say, 'I don't have time,' is like saying, 'I don't want to.'"*
>
> – Lao Tzu, <u>The Art of War</u>

This guide will give insight into what it takes to effectively manage your time, so you can be more efficient in the things that you want to accomplish in your personal life and in your business. Start by measuring your time by how effective it is instead of just by the amount you spent on a task.

It is better to work smarter and not harder by prioritizing your time and your activities to be more task and purpose oriented. Learn when it is time to automate or delegate repetitive tasks. Plan your time and take breaks accordingly to create balance and plan everything. Take control of your time by learning how to leverage your availability to produce the outcome you want to achieve.

$$Availability = Runtime \: / \: Planned \: Production \: Time$$

Disclosure: It is recommended that you seek the advice of a CPA for taxes purposes, a financial advisor for financial purposes, an insurance professional for insurance purposes and the advice of an attorney for legal purposes.

1.
Finding
Time

*O*h, **where did the time go?**

Ever feel like a whole day has passed and you have not managed to accomplish anything? The To Do list keeps getting longer, and deadlines are not getting met? Do you feel like you are being pulled in a million different ways? The people in your personal and work life are demanding your full attention and the clock keeps ticking…

Sounds familiar?

Why is that?

Where is the time going?

How is slipping away…?

The answer might be that you have too many distractions…

How many shows are you watching on your favorite subscription service?

How many hours are you wasting in traffic every day?

"We all have only twenty-four hours in each day" That is a popular saying that we often hear but when we break it down... Do we really?

How do you spend most of that time?

How many hours do you sleep every day?

Most people sleep 7 to 8 hours out..

Do you work?

That might represent another 8 hours of your day.

How much time do you spend preparing and eating the family dinner?

Do you practice sports or go to the gym?

How much time do you spend on family activities or driving your kids to school or after school activities? Do you wish there were more hours in a day?

"The life we receive is not short, but we make it so, nor do we have any lack of it, but are wasteful of it."
—Seneca the Younger, mentioned on the Shortness of Life in 49 A.D.

All those activities take our time away so it is important to spend the remaining hours being intentional. Every minute is precious because once it is gone, you cannot get it back. Dedicate that time to do the things you really want to do!

Time is more valuable than money. You can get more money, but you cannot get more time." ——Jim Rohn

Have you ever wanted to write a book but your busy day got in the way?

Stop trying to find the perfect time. There will never be a better time than right now.

How do other successful people manage to do it?

It is All About Time Management

Take Imperfect Action!!!

Make a simple commitment like Darren Rowse. Darren would get up fifteen minutes earlier each day to write. The result of this was, after three and a half months, he finished his first e-book. The breakdown was fifteen minutes per day, one hundred and five days, twenty-seven hours less of sleep to keep writing, and over $100,000 in profit.

He made a choice to take a small bite out of a big goal no matter how many times he faced the temptation of hitting the snooze button.

> *"Your time is limited, so don't waste it living someone else's life…"*
> —Steve Jobs, the legendary co-founder and former chief executive of Apple Inc.

Tip: Start slow, take it one day at a time, one step at a time, and just START 🏰. Start Lean, and Start Smart.

Manage Your Time,

Don't Let Your Time Manage You!

Some of the benefits of doing so are:

- Feel more in control.

- Increasing your productivity.

- Ability to focus longer on a task.

- Becoming more aware of your habits or distractions.

- Feeling a sense of accomplishment.

- Everything starts by understanding where your time is being spent.

- It is necessary to clearly define your goals.

CREATE AN AUDIT OF YOUR TIME

- Determine the method you are going to use. It can be as simple as a blank piece of paper or any of the apps available in the market that you can choose from to help you.

    - Toggl Track

    - Harvest

    - ATracker

    - TrackingTime

    - RescueTime

- List everything you did from the moment you went up to where you went back to bed.

- Track your time over a period of several days.

- Set an alarm to remind you what needs to be tracked.

- Analyze the data.

Do not use your time audit to increase your to-do list but as a way to eliminate distractions so you can focus on the most important task. Make sure to commit to the improvements.

CREATE A DO NOT LIST

It will help you list the distractions that are robbing your time and getting in the way of you achieving your goals.

DISTRACTION (be specific)	IMPACT (be specific)	MY NOT TO DO LIST	I WILL INSTEAD

TAKE

CONTROL OF

YOUR LIFE!!!

2.
MANAGE
YOUR TIME

*M*anaging your time is the *process of organizing it,* to do different activities at different times during the day so you can be more productive and work smarter by getting more done in less time.

Start managing your time more effectively by:

1. **Consider using an *Eisenhower matrix*** also known as the Urgent-Important Matrix. to help you prioritize your work.

> *"What is important is seldom urgent and what is urgent is seldom important."*
>
> —Dwight D. Eisenhower

He was the 34th president of the United States, and a WWII general that developed this method so he could focus on what was most important to him. Winning the war and running the country!!!

The key is to identify what is important vs what is urgent. Do not spend all your time solving urgent tasks but not taking care of the most important ones.

Priority = Importance x Urgency

The genius of this matrix is that it not only allows you to identify what needs to be done right away but also what needs to be delegated or even completely eliminated from the to-do list of activities.

- Limit to no more that 10 to do task to each quadrant

- Create a separate matrix for your personal and professional task

- Color code it

- Cut the fat, eliminate or delegate the task that not important and urgent

THE EISENHOWER MATRIX

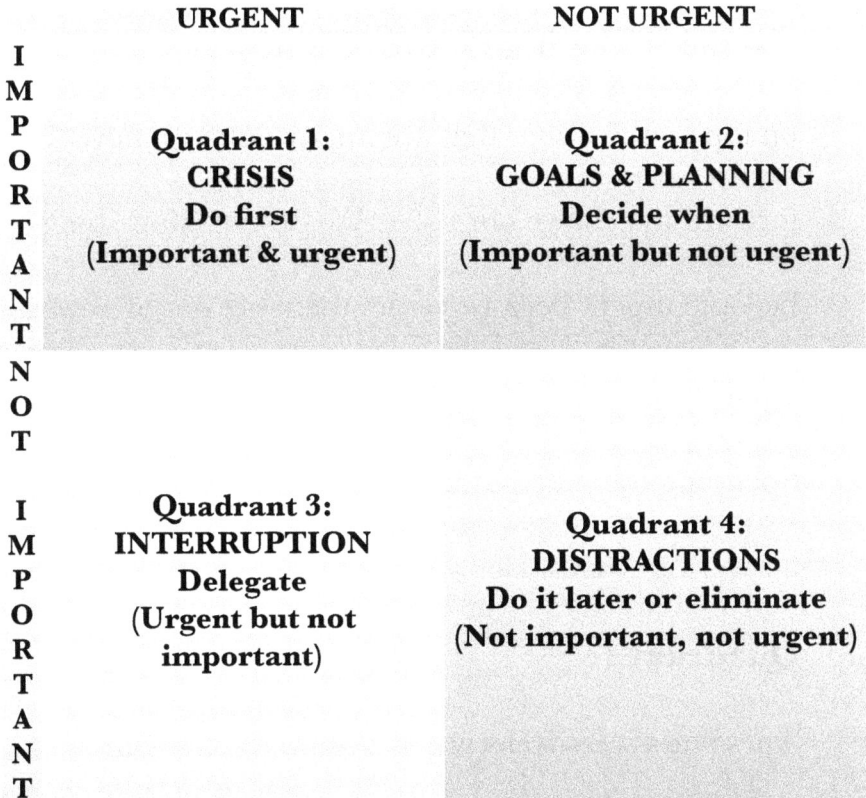

	URGENT	NOT URGENT
IMPORTANT	**Quadrant 1:** **CRISIS** **Do first** **(Important & urgent)**	**Quadrant 2:** **GOALS & PLANNING** **Decide when** **(Important but not urgent)**
NOT IMPORTANT	**Quadrant 3:** **INTERRUPTION** **Delegate** **(Urgent but not important)**	**Quadrant 4:** **DISTRACTIONS** **Do it later or eliminate** **(Not important, not urgent)**

Quadrant 1:

Minimize the time spend in crisis mood. They tend to stress you and suck your energy out. Figure out what needs to be delegated, plan and/or prioritized.

Quadrant 2:

We want to spend the most time in this quadrant that is also called **The Big Picture Quadrant**, where we stay on top of the things that are important and move us forward to achieve our goals. We do not allow things to become urgent because we let them get out of control.

Quadrant 3:

Spending too much time on these tasks, like reading and answering emails. Delegate or reduce the task you can.

Quadrant 4:

These tasks are irrelevant like unproductive time spent on social media or watching excessive TV. Minimize and reduce those activities to reclaim that time for more important task.

2. Identify Your Big Rocks

The big rocks (4 to 5 maximum) are your big priorities that you need to get done in the next 12 month. A term popularized by Stephen Covey in his book "The Seven Habits of Highly Effective People" based in the story of a teacher lecture demonstration in front of his classes.

> "The story says that he filled a one gallon Mason Jar with big rocks. When the jar was full he asked his students if it was full. They responded that yes, so he proceeded to fill it with a sack of gravel and ask them again if it was full. While some responded that yes, others said no. He then took a bag of sand and sifted into the jar on the spaces between the big rocks and the gravel. When he asked again this time,

they responded that it was not, so he proceeded to fill it with water. "

What was the point of this exercise?

It is about learning to identify your big rocks that are getting in the way of achieving your goals.

- Prioritize them before you get distracted by the sand and the gravel.
- Commit time to get then done
- Set clear goals for them
- Set clear metrics to track your progress
- Be honest about your progress
- What could you be doing differently to prioritize your time better?
- What could get in the way?

3. **Consider using an *Action Priority Matrix*** to

decide how much time to dedicate to competing and

demanding tasks. It is a handy tool that can help you when

you are stressed and need help getting things done.

THE ACTION PRIORITY MATRIX

	URGENT	NOT URGENT
I M P A C T **H I G H**	**Quadrant 1:** **Quick Wins** **High Impact, Low Effort**	**Quadrant 2:** **Big Projects** **High Impact, High Effort**
L O W	**Quadrant 3:** **Filler Task** **Low Impact, Low Effort**	**Quadrant 4:** **Hard Slog** **Low Impact, High Effort**

EFFORT

QUICK WINS:

Create a habit of spending 5 minutes brainstorming quick

wins every week.

- Do as many as you can.

- Identify quick wins that you can complete daily or

  weekly.

- Don't avoid the big projects because of the quick wins.

BIG PROJECTS:

- Set time aside to get the big projects done
- Identify everything that would be needed to accomplish your big project
- Set goals with deadlines
- Break down big projects in smaller projects
- Break down big task into smaller task (30- 90 min)
- Identify the order that those smaller tasks need to be done.
- Set aside distractions to focus and increase productivity.

FILLER TASK:

These are administrative tasks that have low impact and require low effort . They take less than 15 minutes to get done. Email is one example of a filler task.

- Chunk blocked similar time together and became more efficient in the way to get them done.

- Minimize or delegate what you can.

- Take care of them when you gaps in your schedule

- Schedule in between more important tasks to give yourself a break.

- Use music to boost your mood

HARD SLOG:

- Eliminate or avoid what you can.

4. Identify your Prime Time

Sam Carpenter coined the biological prime time method in his book "Work the System." It refers to the time during the day where you are more energized, you are hyper focused and can block distractions. It is based on physiology and it is driven by our own body's ultradian rhythms. It is a cycle that repeats throughout our 24 hours days. As natural as our breathing is.

- Determine when your prime time is to devote this time to your most important projects.
- Block this time out on your calendar as a mandatory meeting. Put a "do not disturb sign" on your office door and lock yourself away to avoid interruptions.
- This will be your most productive time. You will be able to accomplish more in two hours of prime time than in any other time during your day.
  - Keep track of your energy levels and high peaks.
  - Use a time tracker

- ***Focus on Intentions instead of outcomes or the tactics*** you would need to employ to achieve the desired results.

- Do not allow interruption during this time.

  - **Capture and Identify:** What needs to be done. Visualize your intentions and goals. Picture yourself in one plus years from now. Visualize your perfect day.

  - **For Long Term Projects - Plan Backward**: Improve your chances of achieving a goal by planning backward. Write down the goal you wish to accomplish and move backwards through the task.

Intentions	Outcome	Tactics
Focus on What you want to accomplish	Close "X" deals to make "Y" in Revenue	Make 100 prospecting calls a week
Visualize it		Schedule demos with new prospects
		Send 100 emails.

These goals might take planning, time and dedication. They can be complicated or challenging, and they might require patience. This process, however, will allow you to see the big picture. It will help you focus on the results and provide the structure to accomplish the task in the right order.

• For Short Term Projects - Plan Forward:

Most of us plan forward, which works well for short-term projects. Break projects down into small goals for a short-term. This also works to help you accomplish big tasks.

    • Be clear of your intentions: Write them down.

5. Learn when it is time to rest.

Elite performers and super high achievers people don't just practice deliberately and persistently, they also *rest* strategically. The same way that our prime time is driven by our own body's ultradian rhythms base. It happens every hour and a half to two hours, the times that we have less energy and we are the most sluggish are driven by the "ultradian dip," Those are the time that we should strategically take breaks or rest instead of working thru it with the use of energy supplements like caffeine, hormones or adrenaline that makes add stress to our bodies.

6. Consider using the Pomodoro Technique:

Developed by Francesco Cirillo in 1980, it is a simple but powerful technique that can help you to:

1. To focus on the task at hand.

2. As a strategy to bust procrastination if you keep finding yourself being easily distracted.

3. Combat avoidance of big and/or intimidating tasks we keep putting off because they are too big or that intimidate you by breaking it down into smaller tasks.

4. Get hyper focus on one activity at a time.

5. Get back in the flow of creativity.

6. Gamify the task by applying each individual section to improve in a task.

7. Plan out each section in advance to optimize the technique.

   • Set a time early in the day to plan the Pomodoro section of the day.

- Analyze how many section each task in your to do list would take

- Bigger tasks break down into smaller tasks.

- Set extra time for the focus section in case you need it.

- If you don't use it, repurpose the remaining time to use for learning.

8. Try extending the allocated 25 minute time to find your optimal focus time.

    A. 25 min focus / 5 min break

    B. 52 min focus / 17 min break

    C. 90 min focus / 20- 30 break

    - Try mixing the time interval according to your energy levels

9. Set a buffer, do not go over 12- 14 focus sections a day.

- Postpone the less important tasks for later in the day.

10. Pay attention to the timer.

    - When the timer goes off, you must get to work in the task assigned.

    - Use an app like todoist, a white eraser board or pen and paper to make you accountable for the time preassigned.

    - If you end up finishing the task before the time is up, then use that remaining time to learn or improve about a skill or developing a scope of knowledge by reading a book or article.

    - Do not break the pattern, when the assigned time is over you must stop working and take the break.

How does it work?

1. Pick something in your list that needs to get done.

2. Set a timer for 25 min.

3. Work in that task until that time is over and mark what got done.

4. Take a 5 min break.

5. Repeat the process.

6. After 4 pomodoro take a longer break, 15-30 min break.

If you end up finishing the task before the time is up, then use that remaining time to learn or improve about a skill or developing a scope of knowledge by reading a book or article.

Figure out what method would work better for you? Try taking the todoist, productivity method quiz to find out which one you better.

3.
SET
GOALS

S*et and use SMART GOALS to help you organize your tasks:*

- **S**pecific

- **M**easurable

- **A**ttainable

- **R**ealistic

- **T**ime-bound

Use **SMART GOALS** to help you organize your lists and tasks. Avoid setting unrealistic goals.

- **Goal 1:** Write and publish fresh content for social media (50%)

- **Goal 2:** Education and mentoring (25%)

- **Goal 3:** Client prospecting (10%)

- Break down your Smart Goals into **Actionable Activities Tasks**.

- Analyze how you are letting the time slip away by conducting an audit of your time. Look back and analyze the major distractions that got in the way and how you actually spent your time.

Create a daily to do list of t tasks that need to be. Use either the traditional pen and paper or an electronic app like: To do list or Trello.

ORGANIZE YOUR LIST OF ACTIVITIES

1. **PRIORITIZE:** What needs to be done? Define the order of importance, category, and due date. Use the ABC type of prioritization or the David Allen's

Getting Things Done (GTD) methodology—

whatever you feel most comfortable with.

    A. **Action:** Prioritize the tasks you need to do, the things you want to do, and the jobs you have to do.

    B. **Waiting for:** Anything pending that you have delegated or are waiting on.

    C. **Projects:** Break down large tasks into smaller actionable steps.

2. **Someday/Maybe:** Anything that you want to accomplish but tasks not requiring your immediate attention.

3. **WRITE DOWN** the tasks and set a hard deadline for completion.

    A. Do the work.

    B. Cross tasks off, one-by-one

Some of the benefits of creating a **TO DO LIST** include:

1. Tasks we haven't done tend to distract us. Making a solid plan to get them done reduces this anxiety.

2. To Do lists give you structure.

    A. They give you a plan and timeline that you can stick with.

    B. They show proof of what you have achieved that day, week, or month.

Use a resource such as Rescue Time, to help you understand how much time you're spending online and also which tools you're using.

Use an electronic calendar or a paper calendar (possibly in a diary) to track your tasks. Create a schedule and allocate time for each task that you want to accomplish. Stick to that time.

4.
Schedule It

*U*se techniques such as Time or Schedule blocking for your days and weeks.

"He who every morning plans the transactions of that day and follows that plan carries a thread that will guide him through the labyrinth of the most busy life."

-Victor Hugo

Some experts recommend allocating yourself two or three times the amount you assume a task will take to accomplish.

Hofstadter's Law:

"It always takes longer than you expect, even when you take into account Hofstadter's Law". (Avis)

Remember to Schedule:

- **Work Time:** Schedule time for prospecting in the mornings when people are less tired. Avoid multitasking.

- **Me Time:** Schedule time for yourself to exercise, meditate, do yoga, read a book, sleep late, or anything else that makes you happy. Define how much time you would need or want for yourself, not to just do things but to be you. Create your own space.

- **Family Time:** Schedule family time, meal preparation, and time with your family.

- **Social Time:** Allow yourself time to relax, let loose, and socialize. Schedule days off, workouts,

- **Learning Time:** Schedule time for education. DON'T FORGET… to schedule your prime time.

- Place buffers in between tasks.

- Schedule time for breaks and meals.

- Focus on one task at a time.

    This simple step will increase your productivity up to 80%.

Say **NO** to projects or people that do not align with your

SMART GOALS, and most importantly, do not feel bad

about saying NO.

5.
Color
Code It

*C*olor Code Your Calendar. It will help you maximize productivity like different colors represent different things to your brain.

- **Grey:** Represents balance. Use gray to highlight your meetings.

- **Red:** Enhances attention to detail. Red is usually associated with danger, mistakes, and caution. Use it to time block for detail-oriented tasks.

- **Purple:** Boosts creativity. We associate purple with creativity, imagination, and wisdom. Use it to time block brainstorming sessions.

- **Blue:** Boosts creativity and relaxation. We associate blue with openness, peace, and tranquility. Blue makes people feel safe about being creative.

- **Pink:** Represents calmness. Use it to block time for breaks.

- **Green:** Represents health and tranquility. Use it to block your lunch break.

- White: Represents happiness and simplicity.

.

6
Eliminate
Or Reduce

Eliminate or reduce the things that have been taking your time. Thing likes constantly checking your email or notifications, social media, and regular mail by:

• Schedule time (an hour) to deal with email, social media, and regular mail.

• Combine similar tasks together.

• Set an "overflow day" to catch up with any tasks you are falling behind on.

• Be flexible. Don't set a schedule so rigid that it is not realistic. You should be able to move things around if there is an emergency.

• Learn what tasks are worth your time and which tasks should be automated or outsourced. Start with those tasks that are time consuming, you don't have the necessary skills to do, or you dread doing.

• Choose to automate repetitive tasks in order to remove time consuming activities from your schedule.

Nowadays, there is an app for everything that you could ever need. It is best to start simple and only use the ones that are best for you and that saves you countless hours in your workflow. Do not automate tasks that require creativity and human input.

- Automate your monthly bills, recurring expenses, and taxes to help save you time and money. Several apps are available such as Hurdlr, Mint, Wave, and Xero.

- Learn to keep track of all your projects in one place and communicate with other members of your team or contractors by using an app such as Asana, Slack, Monday, or Trello.

- Use a calendar app such as Meetingbird, Calendly, or Doodle to automate your appointments, meetings, and events.

- Use an app, such as Buffer or Edgar, to help manage your social media activity for tasks including publishing posts, reposting, and scheduling.

- Create mini automations between your favorite business tools by using Zapier.

1. Outsourcing may cost you more money, but it will save you valuable time. Time that can be better spent on activities that are more important in your life or to grow your business.

"Don't be fooled by the calendar. There are only as many days in the year as you make use of. One person gets only a week's

value out of a year while another gets a full year's value out of a week."

- Charles Richards

Some questions to keep in mind when you outsource to others are:

1. What is the reputation of the person providing the service?

2. What is the scope of the services available?

3. Are they able to deliver the service in the time required?

4. What is their experience and skill level?

5. Do they have a portfolio or work history that enables you to verify their past experience?

6. Do you work well together?

Depending on the task required, nowadays you can hire a virtual assistant across the globe or use freelance marketplace sites. Freelance marketplaces can help find the help you need at an affordable price.

Upwork at www.upwork.com

Freelancer at www.freelancer.com

Peopleperhour at www.peopleperhour.com

Guru at www.guru.com

Toptal at www.toptal.com

Codeable at www.codeable.io

Outsourcely at www.outsourcely.com

Truelancer at www.truelancer.com

Remember to follow your schedule as much as possible but be flexible, adjust your schedule as needed. Create new **SMART GOALS,** and create a system to *TRACK YOUR PROGRESS* in order to stay engaged.

- There are several tools available that you can use for this purpose such as Google Spreadsheet, Excel, or just plain paper. Remember that while digital spreadsheets might be more efficient, they may not give you the same sense of satisfaction as when you write down tasks and check them off as completed.

- Some of the things that you want to track in order to measure progress could be:

- Number of tasks completed.

- Current status (completed, not started, or started).

- Upcoming calendar of daily tasks and appointments.

- Key action items needed to complete each week.

AVOID SELF SABOTAGE!!!

PROCRASTINATION has been classified as a behavioral self-handicapping strategy since the 1970s. It is a self-preservation method we subconsciously use to deal with our fear of failure. This means that we create a handy excuse to deal with our shortcomings by blaming something or someone else.

We are most likely to self-sabotage when tasks are high stakes. Prevent it by:

1. Recognizing that you are procrastinating.

2. Reframing your approach.

3. Breaking down tasks into manageable sizes.

4. Recognize milestones.

5. Avoid assuming you can do more than you can.

Statistically, most people are productive for 2.5 hours a day.

Take Breaks.

It has been proven to improve your productivity, and it can help you refocus your attention. Not only that, it will help you reduce stress, give you a boost of energy and so much more.

A technique called *The 5 Second Rule* by Mel Robbins can help you take breaks. Here's what she says about it in her book:

> *"Anytime there's something you know you should do, but you feel uncertain, afraid, or overwhelmed...just take control by counting backwards 5- 4- 3- 2- 1. That'll quiet your mind. Then, move when you get to 1."*
>
> –Mel Robbins, in The 5 Second Rule

MAKE
YOUR TIME
COUNT

Keep in Touch

Thanks for Reading,

We would love to hear if you have questions, suggestions, inspiring quotes and top tips that have worked for you in using the: **It's All About Time Management©.** *This Book is part of the series:* **"How to Launch the Business that Fits Your Lifestyle©,** *a one stop resource guide to help you get a comprehensive understanding of what is required to build the lifestyle of your dreams.*

Feel free to email me at <u>niurka@amorumbrella.com</u>

Or tweet @amorumbrella

This book and the series is the product of many hearts, and conversations over time. I am forever grateful to all who contributed directly or indirectly, too many to mention all by name but thank you. If you enjoyed this book, please consider leaving an honest review on your favorite store.

Niurka

GET THE
COMPANION BOOKS
IN THE SERIES!

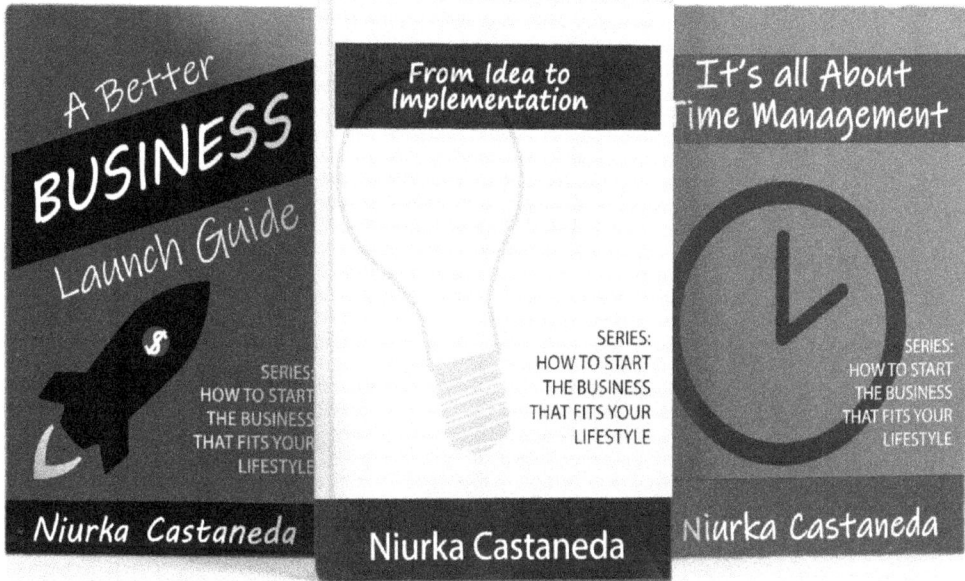

More books coming soon...

Sign up to be notified of new releases, giveaways and pre-release specials -

plus, get a free ebook!

www.amorumbrella.com/free

SERIES: HOW TO
START THE BUSINESS
THAT FITS YOUR LIFESTYLE

by: Niurka Castaneda

The series is a one stop resource guide to help you get a comprehensive understanding of what is required to build the business of your dreams by empowering you with the critical skills, thoughts, feelings, relevant information, actions you need to adopt to be successful in your endeavors. Each book can be read independently of the other ones.

DO YOU KNOW SOMEONE WHO IS AN ENTREPRENEUR IN THE MAKING?

Give them the gift that will help them get a huge jump start in their

entrepreneurial journey, and increase their odds of success.

Author's Niurka Castaneda' passion project, **"How to Start the**

Business that Fits Your Lifestyle©" book series is designed to give the

reader three things:

1.   Confirmation that they are ready or not to become an entrepreneur.

2.   A glimpse of their life as an entrepreneur.

3.   A clear simple path to become an entrepreneur.

BOOK ORDER FORM

Niurka Castaneda,
Author & Empowerment Coach,
Miami, FL 33177
(786) 445-2364
founderstime.com

Bulk orders are available!

Print Full Name:

Cell Phone:

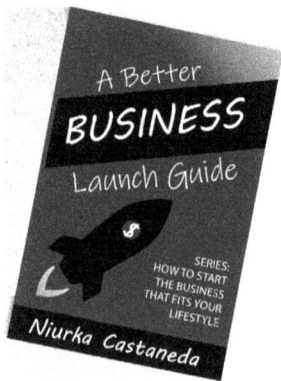

SERIES: HOW TO
START THE BUSINESS
THAT FITS YOUR LIFESTYLE

A Better Business
Launch Guide

by: Niurka Castaneda

Starting a business involves planning, making key financial decisions, and completing a series of legal activities. **A Better Business Launch Guide**© will take you through an A to Z action plan process on how to get your business up and off the ground, as well as, giving you the tools to start building the foundation of your own entrepreneurial dreams.

BOOK ORDER FORM

Niurka Castaneda,
Author & Empowerment Coach,
Miami, FL 33177
(786) 445-2364
founderstime.com

Bulk orders are available!

Print Full Name:

Cell Phone:

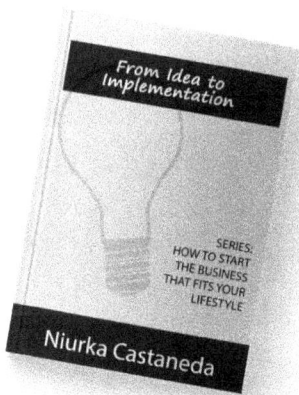

SERIES: HOW TO
START THE BUSINESS
THAT FITS YOUR LIFESTYLE

From Idea to
Implementation

by: Niurka Castaneda

Whether you are exploring a new idea or new endeavor, **From Idea to Implementation**© will guide you in how to get it out of your head, organize it and transform it into a tangible product or service that you can hear, see, and/or touch. In addition, it will give you the tools to unlock the power of your creativity to start developing, testing, and bringing your ideas to market.

BOOK ORDER FORM

Niurka Castaneda,
Author & Empowerment Coach,
Miami, FL 33177
(786) 445-2364
founderstime.com

Bulk orders are available!

Print Full Name:

Cell Phone:

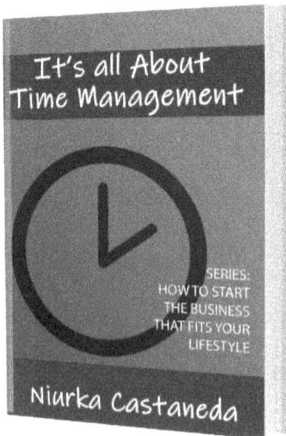

SERIES: HOW TO
START THE BUSINESS
THAT FITS YOUR LIFESTYLE

It's all About
Time Management
by: Niurka Castaneda

Starting a business involves planning, making key financial decisions, investing your time and resources in an efficient way that allows you to grow. **It's All about Time Management**© will take you through simple practical steps to figure out when you are the most productive on specific tasks and allow you to create a framework for optimal productivity that can help you master your time. It will also provide the necessary strategies & tools to work smarter and get more done in less time.

REGISTER FOR THE COMPANION ON DEMAND COURSE IN THE SERIES!

This mini-course will take you from steps A to Z on how to get your business up and off the ground.

Topics Covered

- How to create your business name
- Get your business Lic
- Business Address
- Business Insurance
- Domain names
- And special certifications

Register for the course

FOR ADDITIONAL HELP
& INFORMATION

My goal is to help you be successful in your entrepreneurial journey and

get everything you want from your lifestyle business by offering three ways

to help you fully and purely implement.

1.   Self Implementation

2.   Supported Self Implementation

3.   Professional Implementation

You can find out more about these three approaches, download

free tools, subscribe to our blog for regular helpful tips, find out how to

become a professional certified implementer, and schedule seminars,

workshops and speaking engagement in our websites: founderstime.com &

amorumbrella.com

EMPOWERMENT SERIES

Niurka Castaneda,
Author & Empowerment Coach,
Miami, FL 33177
(786) 445-2364
founderstime.com

Just the thought of starting a business is exciting, but it can quickly become overwhelming when you are trying to get started. Where do you start? An excellent place is here. You seek out information and it can be information overload! The following services are offered based on the specific needs of the client. All services are offered in both English and Spanish. Please place a check next to all services you will be receiving from Ventures C & A LLC.

Training topics are taught via:
* Seminars & Workshops
* One one one coaching sections
* Tele, zoom seminars or Webinars
* Consultations

All training programs can be customized to fit the customer's needs.

ENTREPRENEURSHIP TRAINING		
How to Launch Your Idea	Are you ready to explore what building a lifestyle out of your ideas that represents your passions, skills and talents could look like for you? Get the strategies and tools you need that would help you get your ideas out of your head and provide an action game plan to turn them into a reality.	

EMPOWERMENT SERIES		
How to Write & Publish Your First Book	The strategies and tools you need to empower you in the process of telling your story. Aspiring authors will learn how to write, publish, promote, distribute and sell your own book.	
Creative Entrepreneurship	Learn exercises to help you and your team overcome the common barriers to creativity. Through hands-on activities designed and practiced by creative experts, you'll gain practical skills to help you learn from failure, find inspiration, and get unstuck. Gain the tools and mindsets to break patterns, generate new ideas, and take creative leaps. Increase your creative problem-solving skills with exercises you can use again and again. Break through creative blocks and generate new ideas by embracing a creative mindset.	
How to Bootstrap your Business	Get practical frameworks you can use to grow your small business using lean practices that will help you save money, time and avoid pitfalls common to build and grow a business that serves you.	
How to Get Your Business to Stand Out and Be Visible	Learn how to steal the spotlight by ranking higher in google search, going viral on social media, and outshining your competitors.	

EMPOWERMENT SERIES

How to Fund Your Business	We will guide you in how to best navigate the process of securing funding to launch and expand your business. Learn about the do's and don'ts, the opportunities and the obstacles of obtaining funding for your business.	
How to Stay Outside The Box, & Inside The Budget	Everything we're used to has changed. Like any rules of improvisation, constraints actually help us be more creative. We will show you how to look at your changing budget and new work restrictions as useful tools to keep your creativity flowing during this time of uncertainty.	
How to Fix Your Credit	Credit impacts all our lives in a big way. Unfortunately, the topic is rarely explained very clearly. We're here to fix that! Everything repair companies do for you and charge huge recurring monthly fees, you can honestly do yourself with the right knowledge. Be ready to learn, and most importantly, please be PREPARED TO CHANGE YOUR FINANCIAL LIFE! Time is of the essence!!	
How to Find & Win Grants for Your Business	We will guide you in how to best navigate the process of securing grants to launch and expand your business.	

EMPOWERMENT SERIES	
How to Manage Your Inventory	Inventory Management is a a crucial piece of a business's profitability. It involves ordering, stocking and using a business's materials or products. Learn how to prioritize, track and practice the 80/20 rule to your inventory to help you understand what you need to order or manufacture more frequently so you can continuously fulfill your customers' needs.
How to Create & Manage Your Supply Chain	We will go over the key benefits to create an extended value supply chain for your small business. We will discuss the key building blocks of Supply chain collaboration including Demand Planning, New Product Development process, order fulfillment, and integrated business planning (S&OP).
Women Stealing the Show	Women's insights are changing the business world. Now is the time to know the power of your ideas, and to trust what you have to offer. Women's workshops in an all-female atmosphere give women a safe and fun place to practice finding their voice... and use it!
How to Get Featured in the Media	Getting in the press, on radio or TV can be a huge boost. Become the leader in your field. Learn how to get featured in podcast, tv, magazines . Get more attention for your business.

EMPOWERMENT SERIES ORDER FORM

Niurka Castaneda,
Author & Empowerment Coach,
Miami, FL 33177
(786) 445-2364
founderstime.com

Print Full Name:	
Cell Phone:	
Email:	

The following services are offered based on the specific needs of the client. All services are offered in both English and Spanish. Please place a check next to all services you will be receiving from Ventures C & A LLC. All training programs can be customized to fit the customer's needs.

CONSULTATION		
	$75.00	Thirty Minute Section
	$150.00	(1 Hour section)
Individual Consultation	$350.00	4 weeks coaching program
		Customized coaching program (5, 6 or 8 weeks)

EMPOWERMENT SERIES ORDER FORM

COACHING		
Telephone or Virtual Coaching	$125.00	(1 Hour section)
Telephone or Virtual Coaching	$125.00	(1 Hour section)
Telephone or Virtual Coaching	$575.00	4 weeks coaching program
		Customized coaching program (5, 6 or 8 weeks)
WORKSHOPS & TRAINING CLASSES		
In House Group Workshop	$125.00	Per person x 5 hrs
Off site group Workshop (1 section)	$175.00	Per person x 5 hrs
INDIVIDUAL PRESENTATION		
Individual Presentation	$1,400.00	2 hr
	$2,250.00	Half day training class
	$3,700.00	Full day training class
		Customized training classes, seminars & workshops (Prices vary according to customer needs)

Special Cooperative pricing for Non profits Organization, Libraries, Schools, Colleges and Universities, Churches and Business Organization
* Outside Geographical Boundaries, Travel Expenses will apply.

BIBLIOGRAPHY

5 benefits of taking breaks. UCL. (2020, September 17). Retrieved January 1, 2022, from https://www.ucl.ac.uk/students/news/2020/feb/5-benefits-taking-breaks

8 Best Fiverr Alternatives in 2021 (better freelance sites). Website Rating. (2021, December 25). Retrieved January 1, 2022, from https://www.websiterating.com/productivity/best-fiverr-alternatives/

About the Author Christine Carter Christine Carter, & Carter, C. C. C. (n.d.). *The quiet secret to success*. Greater Good. Retrieved September 3, 2022, from https://greatergood.berkeley.edu/article/item/the_quiet_secret_to_success

Avis, H. J. (n.d.). Childhood initiated statin therapy in familial hypercholesterolemia. Retrieved from https://pure.uva.nl/ws/files/1691808/126439_02.pdf.

Batto, S., Jane Alexander, & Alisoncross. (2015, December 29). *Treasure mapping*. Jane Alexander. Retrieved September 4, 2022, from https://www.exmoorjane.com/treasure-mapping/

Boogaard, K. (2021, November 30). *Discover your most productive hours with the biological prime time method*. A blog for teams by Trello. Retrieved September 3, 2022, from https://blog.trello.com/biological-prime-time-method

Business News Daily. (n.d.). Retrieved January 1, 2022, from https://www.refer-em.com/11231-how-to-outsource-effectively.html

Calculate OEE. OEE. (n.d.). Retrieved January 1, 2022, from https://www.oee.com/calculating-oee/

Emma-Louise, Contributing Author: Emma-Louise Elsey, Allie Gorman-Jones April 25, Sophia Brown February 22, Emma-Louise February 22, & Name*. (2022, January 5). *Coaching tools 101: The urgent important matrix - what is it and how to use it!* The Coaching Tools Company. Retrieved September 3, 2022, from https://www.thecoachingtoolscompany.com/coaching-tools-101-what-is-the-urgent-important-matrix/

Esposito, E. (2021, December 2). *5 best time tracking apps of 2022*. Zapier. Retrieved September 3, 2022, from https://zapier.com/blog/best-time-tracking-apps/

Gass, N. (2020, January 23). *7 time management tips for entrepreneurs*. Smart Money Mamas. Retrieved January 1, 2022, from https://smartmoneymamas.com/7-time-management-tips-for-entrepreneurs/

Guardian News and Media. (2017, May 10). *The psychology of the to-do list – why your brain loves ordered tasks*. The Guardian. Retrieved January 1, 2022, from https://www.theguardian.com/lifeandstyle/2017/may/10/the-psychology-of-the-to-do-list-why-your-brain-loves-ordered-tasks

How to do a time audit. Lucidchart. (2020, June 25). Retrieved September 3, 2022, from https://www.lucidchart.com/blog/how-to-do-a-time-audit

How to hack your to-do list. YouTube. (2013, February 20). Retrieved January 1, 2022, from https://youtu.be/Xduzwk04l2E

How to overcome procrastination with the Eisenhower Matrix. Lucidchart. (2020, September 16). Retrieved September 3, 2022, from https://www.lucidchart.com/blog/eisenhower-matrix

Journal of Personality and Social Psychology. (n.d.). Retrieved January 1, 2022, from https://users.wfu.edu/masicaej/MasicampoBaumeister2011JPSP.pdf

MacKay, B. J. (2020, May 8). *Time Management Tips & Strategies: 25 powerful ways to be more efficient*. RescueTime Blog. Retrieved January 1, 2022, from https://blog.rescuetime.com/time-management/

Marchese, L. (2021, January 8). How checklists train your brain to be more productive and goal-oriented. A blog for teams by Trello. Retrieved March 1, 2022, from https://blog.trello.com/the-psychology-of-checklists-why-setting-small-goals-motivates-us-to-accomplish-bigger-things

McCloskey, H. (2021, January 7). *How to create more time: A strategy for finally getting ahead of your to-do list*. A blog for teams by Trello. Retrieved January 1, 2022, from https://blog.trello.com/how-to-create-more-time-to-do-list-strategy

Nevins, M. (2022, April 14). *What are your big rocks?* Forbes. Retrieved September 3, 2022, from https://www.forbes.com/sites/hillennevins/2020/01/21/what-are-your-big-rocks/?sh=1215bb5efae3

Robbins, M. (2019). Summary "the 5 second rule by Mel Robbins. Bestof.me.

ScienceDaily. (2009, February 6). *Effect of colors: Blue boosts creativity, while red enhances attention to detail*. ScienceDaily. Retrieved January 1, 2022, from https://www.sciencedaily.com/releases/2009/02/090205142143.htm

Search listening tool for market, Customer & Content Research. AnswerThePublic. (n.d.). Retrieved January 1, 2022, from https://answerthepublic.com/

Seneca, L. A., Nuttall, C. C. D., Seneca, L. A., Seneca, L. A., & Seneca, L. A. (2005). *On the shortness of life: Life is long if you know how to use it.* Penguin Books.

Start here - austinlchurch.com: Advice, courses, and coaching for freelancers. AustinLChurch.com | Advice, Courses, and Coaching for Freelancers. (2021, September 12). Retrieved January 1, 2022, from https://austinlchurch.com/hire-me

the Mind Tools Content Team By the Mind Tools Content Team, Team, the M. T. C., wrote, M., wrote, B. T., & wrote, muhammmadt2. (n.d.). *What is time management?: Working Smarter to enhance productivity.* Time Management Skills From MindTools.com. Retrieved September 3, 2022, from https://www.mindtools.com/pages/article/newHTE_00.htm

Top 10 ways for effective time management for the dental ... (n.d.). Retrieved January 1, 2022, from https://www.dentistryiq.com/dentistry/endodontics/article/16360105/top-10-ways-for-effective-time-management-for-the-dental-executive

TZU, S. U. N. (2022). *Art of war.* HERO.

THE AUTHOR

Photo© Christine Marie Sanchez

Niurka Castaneda grew up in Cuba and comes from a family of entrepreneurs and artists. She is the mom of two incredible kids and has a passion for art, music, reading, travel, photography, and all things positive. Upon immigrating to Miami, she joined and honorably served in the US Military. Today she is a proud Veteran entrepreneur, author, independent filmmaker and producer. She is an advocate for Entrepreneurial initiatives and under the umbrella of her company Amor Umbrella, she focuses on education, media and brand awareness to help inspire, ignite and educate other entrepreneurs on their own entrepreneurial journey.

Learn more about her @ NiurkaCastaneda.com

READ MORE BOOKS BY THE AUTHOR

La Mejor Guía para Comenzar un Negocios

Todo es Cuestión de Manejar tu Tiempo

De la Idea al Éxito

Short Stories/ Travel/ Photojournalism/ Adventure

Venture into the Everglades

- Co written by Masha Andreoni, LCSW & Niurka Castaneda

Aventurarse en el Everglades

- Co escrito por Masha Andreoni, LCSW & Niurka Castaneda

Other books

The Complete Life Reference Guide

- Co written with multiple authors

-

www.ingramcontent.com/pod-product-compliance
Lightning Source LLC
Chambersburg PA
CBHW050513210326
41521CB00011B/2444